The Life Cycle of an

ANT

Trevor Terry &
Margaret Linton

Illustrated by
Jackie Harland

Editor: Penny McDowell

First published in 1987 by
Wayland (Publishers) Limited
61 Western Road, Hove
East Sussex, BN3 1JD, England

British Library Cataloguing in Publication Data
Terry, Trevor
    The life cycle of an ant.—(Life cycles).
    1. Ants—Juvenile literature
        I. Title   II. Linton, Margaret,
        III. Series
        595.79′6   QL568.F7

ISBN 1 85210 117 2

Typeset in the UK by DP Press Limited, Sevenoaks, Kent
Printed and bound by Casterman S.A., Belgium

Notes for parents and teachers
Each title in this series has been specially written and
designed as a first natural history book for young readers.
For less able readers there are introductory captions,
while the more detailed text explains each illustration.

Contents

Where do ants live?   4

Ants live together   6

Young queens and males   8

The queen starts a nest   10

The queen lays her eggs   12

The eggs hatch   14

Worker ants are born   16

Working ants   18

The worker ants and the queen   20

The nest in summer   22

New queens and males   24

The queens and males fly off   26

Keeping ants   28

The life cycle of an ant   30

Glossary   31

Finding out more   31

Index   32

All the words that are
in **bold** are explained in
the glossary on page 31.

Where do ants live?

Ants are busy little **insects**. They live in nests. Different kinds of ants build in different kinds of places. Some ants make small hills in meadows or woods. Others build under stones and paving slabs.

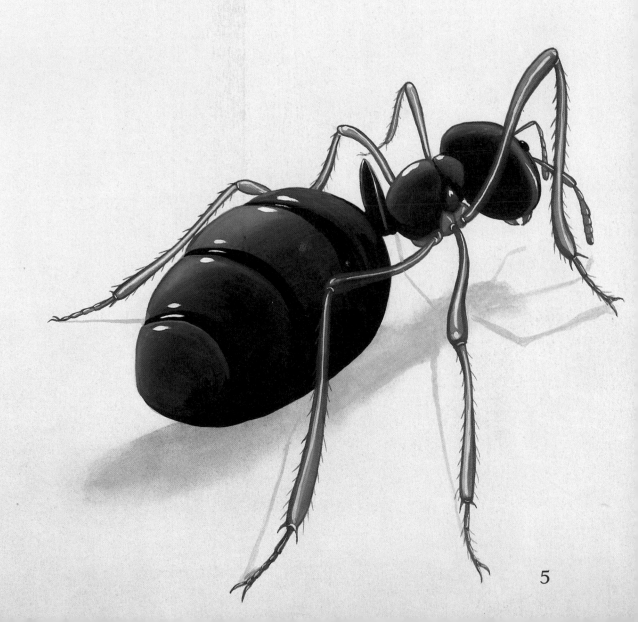

The ants live together.

Ants live and work together just like we do. A **queen ant, male ants** and **worker ants** all live in one nest. The queen is the biggest. She lays the eggs. The worker ants are tiny. They do all the work. There may be thousands of ants in one nest.

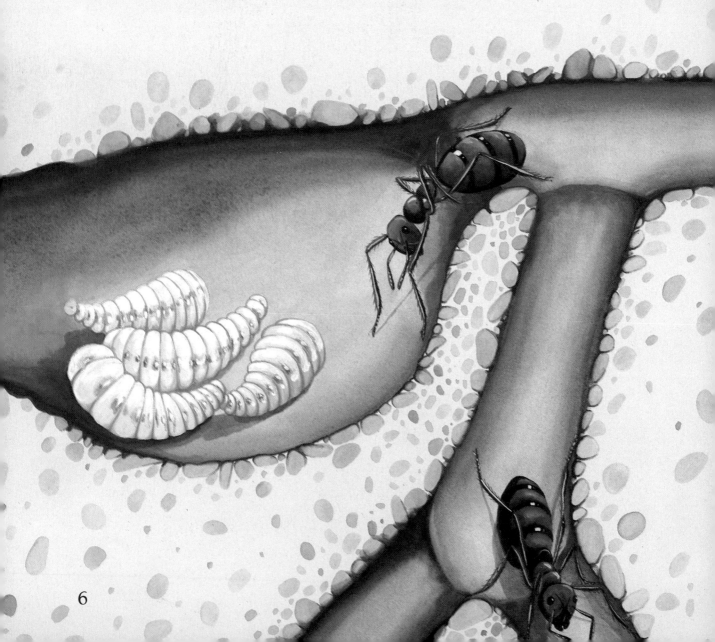

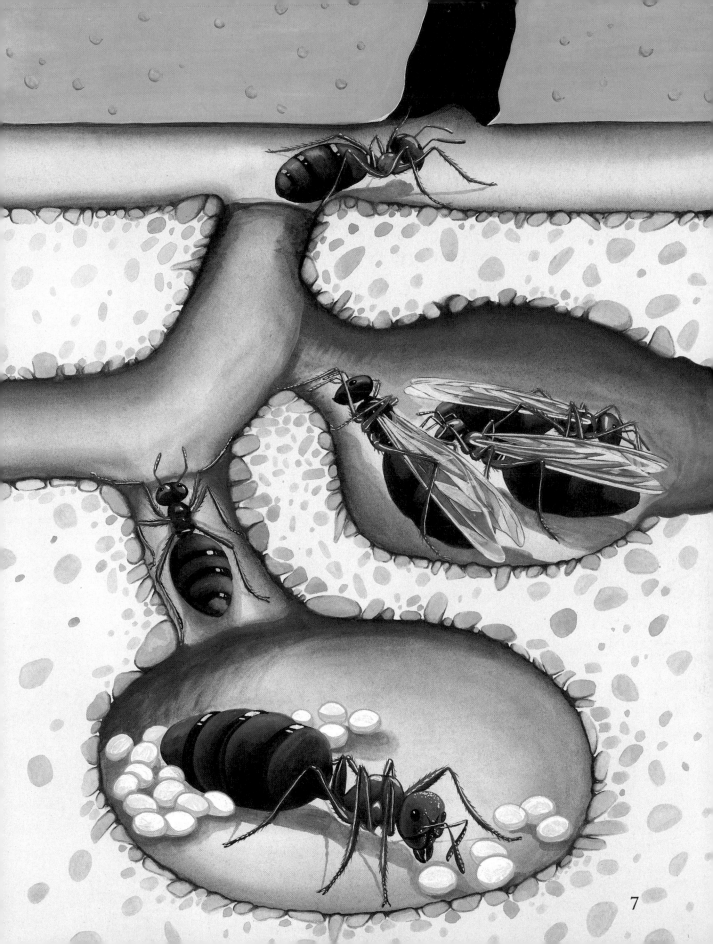

8

Young queens and males fly off.

On a warm day in summer, young queens and male ants fly up into the sky to **mate**. This is called the **marriage flight**. After the marriage flight, the male ants die. Now the young queen ants get ready to lay their first eggs.

The queen ant starts a new nest.

First of all, young queen ants look for good places to build their nests. They will stay there for the rest of their lives. When a queen has found the right place, she breaks off her wings. Then she begins to dig. She makes a small tunnel under the ground.

The first eggs are laid by the queen.

When the tunnel is ready, the queen lays her first eggs. As the weather gets colder, the queen goes to sleep. She stays asleep all winter. She wakes up in the spring and begins to look after her eggs. She licks them to keep them clean.

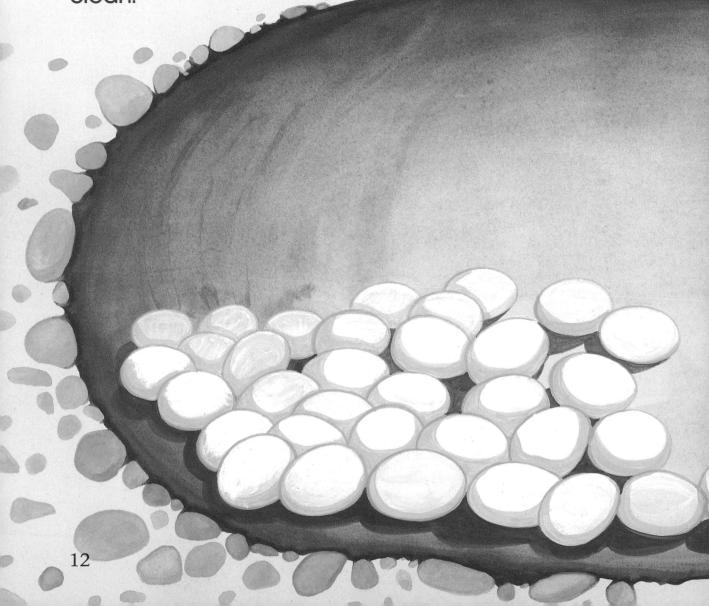

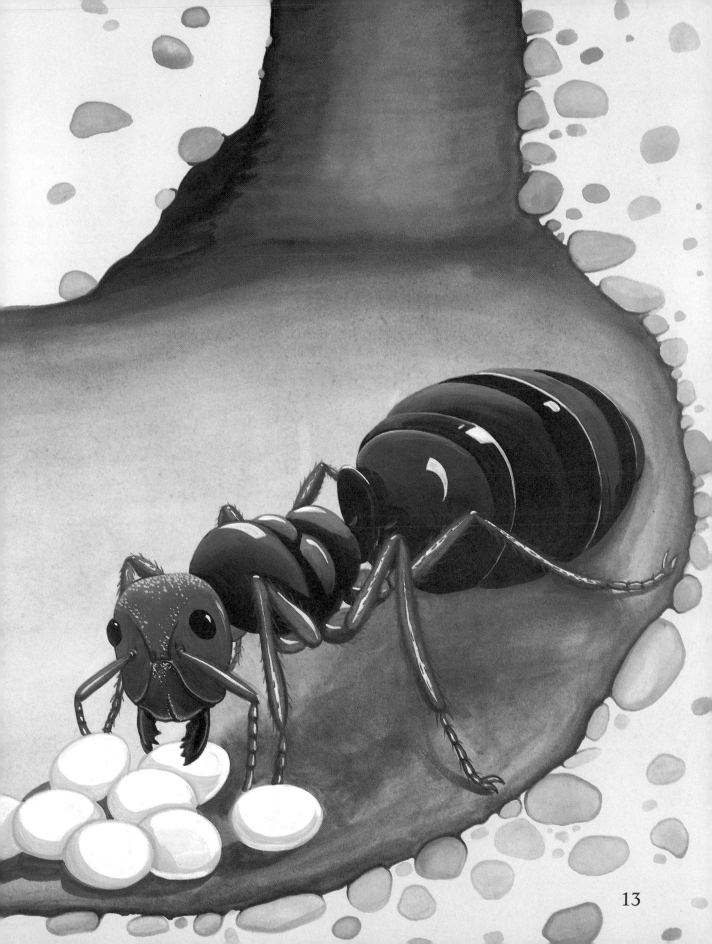

The eggs begin to hatch.

After a few weeks the eggs hatch into white **grubs** called **larvae**. Each **larva** has a soft body, a mouth and tiny sharp jaws. The queen feeds them. The larvae grow very quickly. They grow too big for their skins. The old skins drop off and new skins grow. This is called **moulting**.

New worker ants are born.

Soon the larvae are fully grown. Each larva makes a case around itself, called a **cocoon**. The larva inside the cocoon becomes a **pupa**. After a while the pupa changes into a young worker ant. The queen helps the young ants to come out of their cocoons.

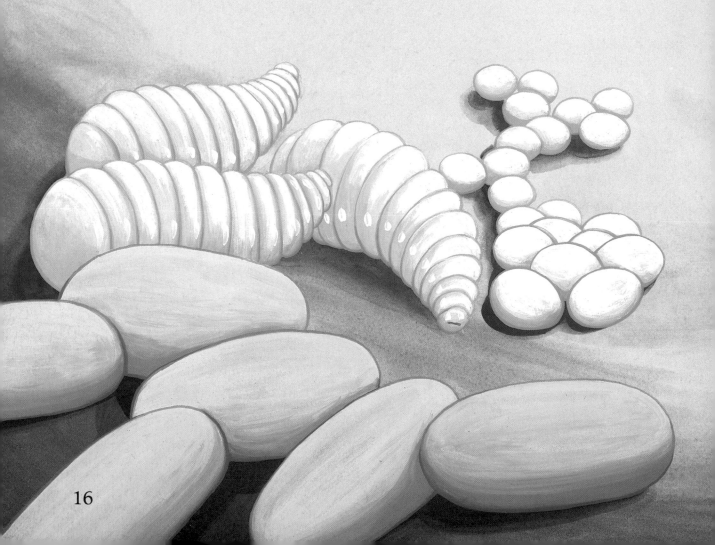

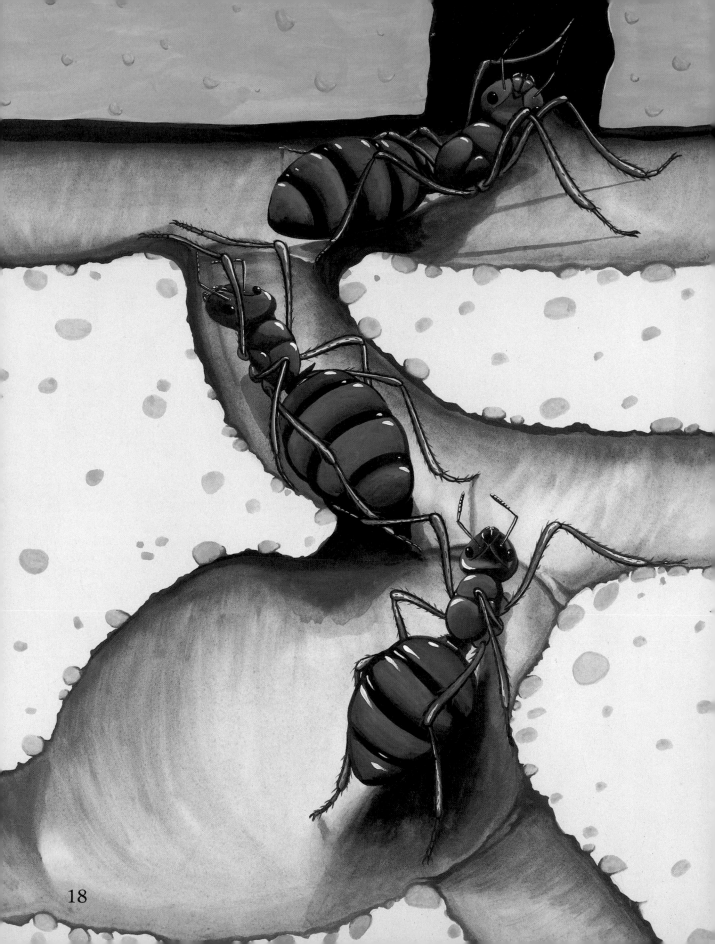

The worker ants begin to work.

The new ants have soft, pale skins. Soon they begin to change. Their colour turns darker. Their skins get harder. They begin to do all kinds of jobs. Some go out to look for food. Ants like drops of sweet juice called honeydew. Honeydew is made by insects called **aphids**.

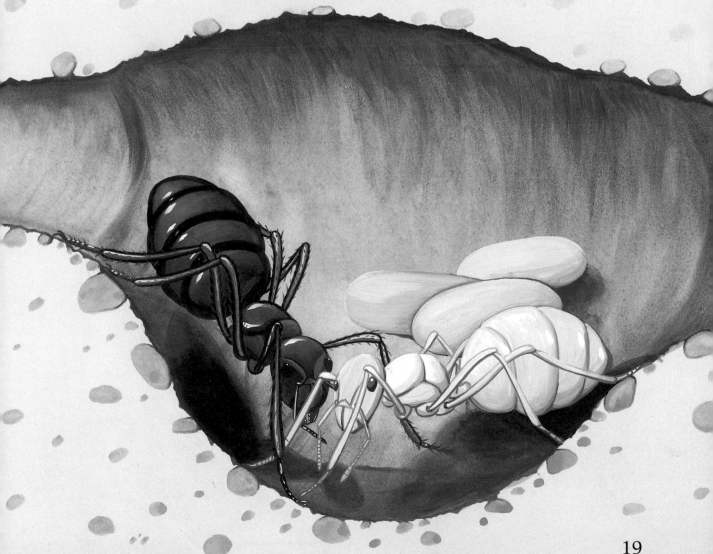

The worker ants look after the queen.

Some worker ants begin to look after the queen. They feed her by putting food from their own mouths into her mouth. They lick her to keep her clean. All this time the queen has been laying more and more eggs. There are more and more larvae and cocoons in the nest.

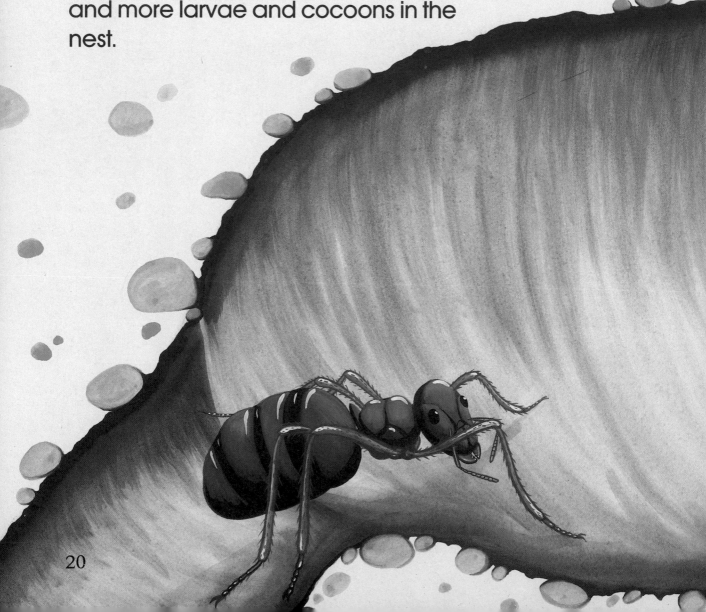

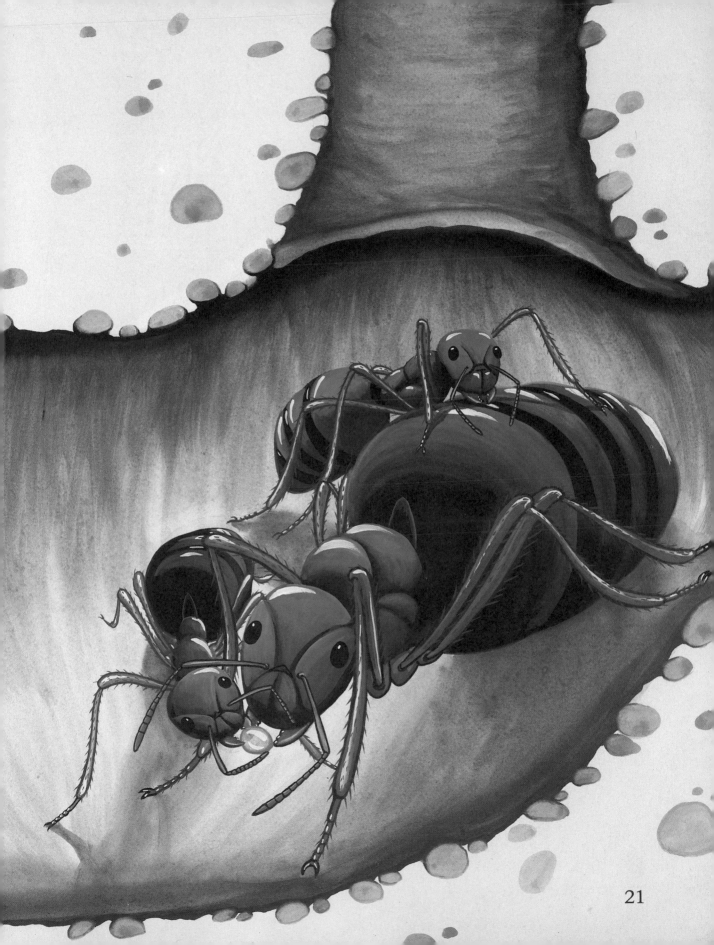

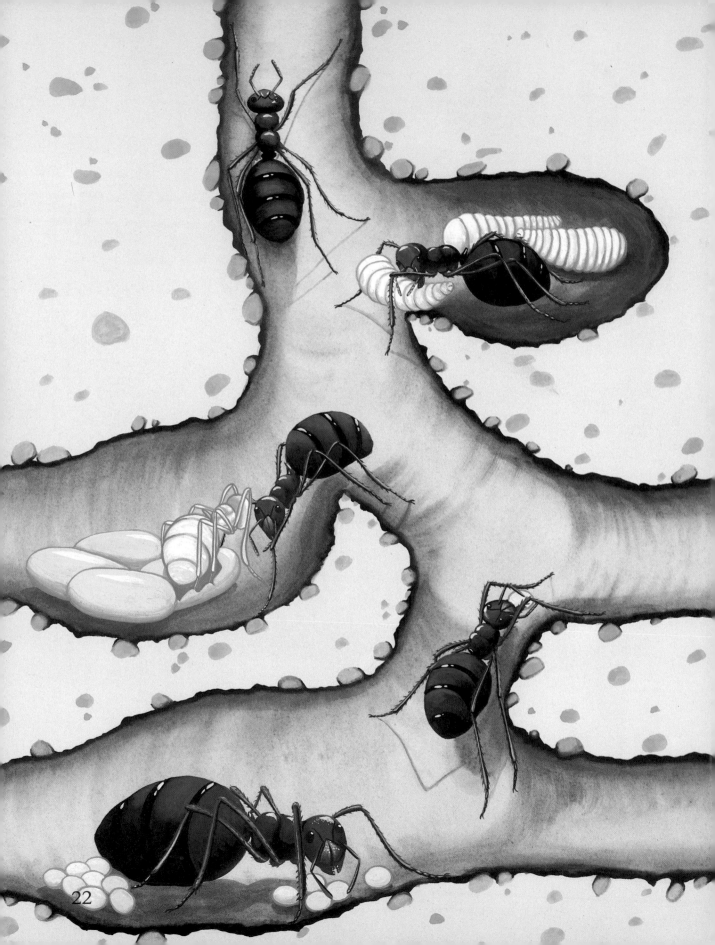

The nest is busy in the summer.

The ants build more tunnels in the summer. They keep the nest clean and tidy. Some worker ants leave the nest to look for food. Others feed the larvae and young ants. **Nurse ants** move the eggs, larvae and cocoons to different parts of the nest.

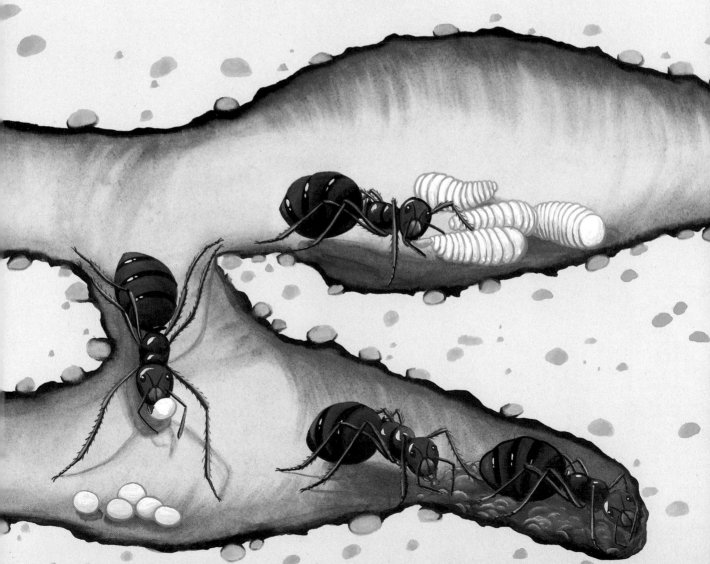

Here are the new queens and males.

During the summer the queen lays some different eggs. These eggs will turn into male ants and young queen ants. The larvae are bigger. The workers feed them on special food. The male ants and young queen ants have wings. They are bigger than the worker ants.

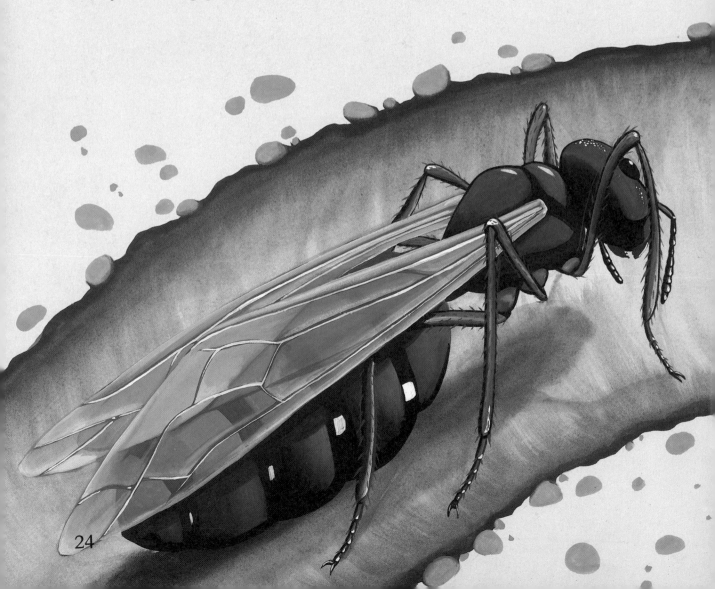

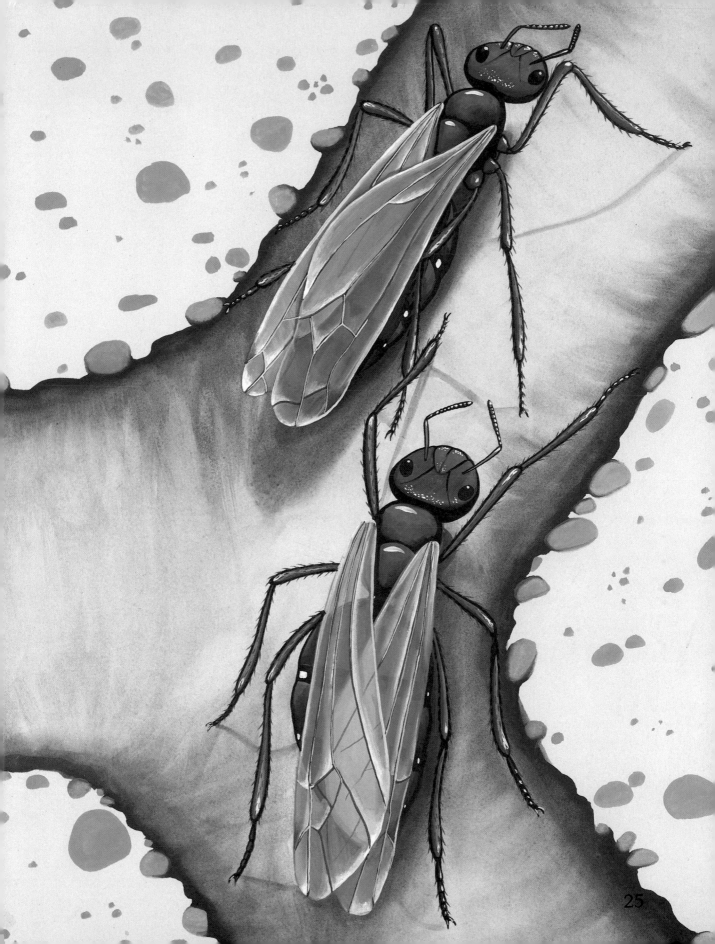

The queens and males are ready to fly.

On a warm day in summer, the males and young queens come out from the nest. Worker ants come out too, and they all scurry around. Then the males and young queens fly up into the sky for the marriage flight. Now the story begins all over again.

Keeping your own ants.

You could make an ants' nest like the one in the picture. Put some moist soil in a large jam jar. Stand the jar in a dish of water to stop the ants getting out. Look under big stones and find some garden ants. Ask an adult to help you. Put the ants in the jar. Cover it with a piece of plywood or hardboard which has a hole in the middle.

Spread a little honey on a small piece
of bark. Put this on top of the cover. Ants
will eat cake crumbs, too. Ants do not
like light, so cover the dish and the jar
with a cardboard box. After a few days,
take the box off. See if the ants have
started to make their tunnels.
Remember to put the box back again.

The life cycle of an ant.

How many stages of the life cycle can you remember? Here is the life cycle of a queen ant.

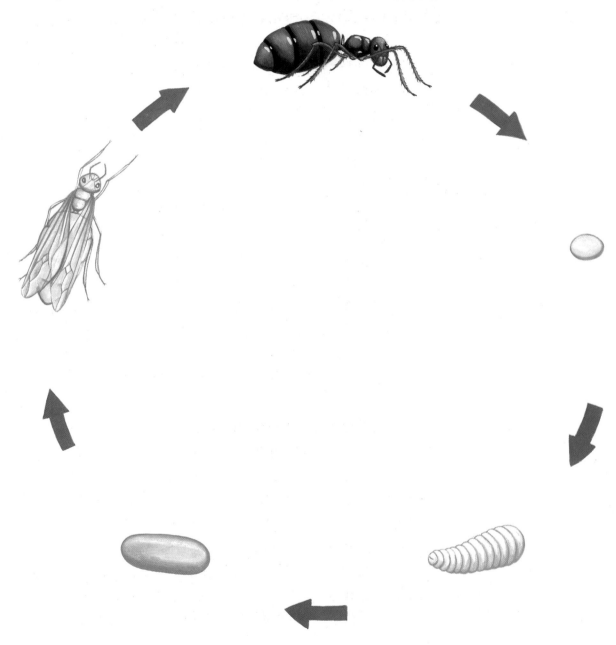

Glossary

Aphids Small insects which suck juices from plants for food.

Cocoon The case which surrounds a pupa.

Grub The larva of an insect, like beetles.

Insects Small animals without a backbone. They have three pairs of legs, and usually two pairs of wings. Their bodies are covered by a hard skin.

Larvae Grubs which hatch from an egg. One grub is called a **larva**. Lots of grubs are called **larvae**.

Male ants Ants which mate with young queens during the marriage flight.

Marriage flight The time when young queens and male ants leave the nest and fly away to mate.

Mate This is when male (father) and female (mother) animals join together. This is how a baby animal is made.

Moulting When the caterpillar (or larva) gets too big for its skin. The old skin comes off and a new skin grows.

Nurse ants Ants who help the queen ant to look after her eggs. They also move the larvae and cocoons around the nest.

Pupa A resting stage when a larva changes into an adult insect.

Queen ant The female ant which lays eggs.

Worker ants Small female ants without wings. They do different jobs in the nest.

Finding out more

Here are some books to read to find out more.

Animal Homes by Malcolm Penny (Wayland, 1987)
Ants by Ralph Whitlock (Wayland, 1979)
Ants by P. & H. Clay (A. & C. Black, 1984)
Discovering Ants by Christopher O'Toole (Wayland, 1986)
Small Garden Animals by Terry Jennings (Oxford, 1981)
The Wildlife in Your Home by Terry Jennings
   (Young Library, 1984)

Index

cocoon   16, 20, 23

eggs   8, 12, 15, 20, 23, 24

food   15, 19, 20, 29

hatching   15

insects   5

larvae   15, 16, 20, 23

male ants   6, 8, 24, 26
marriage flight   8, 26
mate   8
moulting   15

nests   5, 6, 11, 20, 23, 28

nurse ants   23

paving slabs   5
pupa   16

queen ant   6, 8, 11, 12, 15, 16, 20, 24, 26

sleep   12
spring   12
summer   8, 23, 24, 26

tunnels   11, 23, 29

wings   11, 24
winter   12
worker ants   6, 16, 19, 20, 23, 26

Gr. 1 - 3
Ants
Life Cycle
Glossary
Contents
Index
Science